The Battle of the
Little Bighorn

MaryLee Knowlton and Michael V. Uschan

Gareth Stevens Publishing
A WORLD ALMANAC EDUCATION GROUP COMPANY

With all my love to James and John Mike Bloedel – M. V. U.

Please visit our web site at: www.garethstevens.com
For a free color catalog describing Gareth Stevens Publishing's list of high-quality
books and multimedia programs, call 1-800-542-2595 (USA) or 1-800-387-3178
(Canada). Gareth Stevens Publishing's fax: (414) 332-3567.

Library of Congress Cataloging-in-Publication Data

Knowlton, MaryLee.
    The Battle of the Little Bighorn / by MaryLee Knowlton and Michael V. Uschan.
      p. cm. — (Events that shaped America)
    Summary: A description of the 1876 Battle of the Little Bighorn, in which Sioux Indians
defeated General Custer's forces, as well as the events leading up to the confrontation and its
impact afterwards.
    Includes bibliographical references and index.
    ISBN 0-8368-3222-1 (lib. bdg.)
    1. Little Bighorn, Battle of the, Mont., 1876—Juvenile literature. [1. Little Bighorn,
Battle of the, Mont., 1876.] I. Uschan, Michael V., 1948- II. Title. III. Series.
E83.876.K56   2002
973.8'2—dc21   2002021052

This North American edition first published in 2002 by
Gareth Stevens Publishing
A World Almanac Education Group Company
330 West Olive Street, Suite 100
Milwaukee, WI 53212 USA

This edition © 2002 by Gareth Stevens Publishing.

Produced by Discovery Books
Editor: Sabrina Crewe
Designer and page production: Sabine Beaupré
Photo researcher: Sabrina Crewe
Maps and diagrams: Stefan Chabluk
Gareth Stevens editorial direction: Mark J. Sachner
Gareth Stevens art direction: Tammy Gruenewald
Gareth Stevens production: Susan Ashley

Photo credits: Buffalo Bill Historical Center: cover, pp. 4, 23; Corbis: pp. 7, 16, 22, 27;
Granger Collection: pp. 8–9, 20, 25 (top); National Park Service, Little Bighorn Battlefield
National Monument: pp. 5, 19, 24, 25 (bottom); Nebraska State Historical Society: p. 6;
North Wind Picture Archives: pp. 10, 11, 12, 13, 17, 26; Rushmore Photo and Gift: p. 14.

Printed in the United States of America

1 2 3 4 5 6 7 8 9 06 05 04 03 02

Contents

A Battle on the Plains

It was June 25, 1876, a bright, hot day. By the Little Bighorn River in Montana Territory, a huge force of Plains Indian warriors swept down on a small group of about 210 U.S. soldiers from the Seventh **Cavalry** led by Lieutenant Colonel George Armstrong Custer. In two short hours, all the soldiers were dead.

Other Names for the Battle

This was a part of the Battle of the Little Bighorn, the part known as Custer's Last Stand. White people gave it this name in honor of the dead leader. Indians called it the Battle of the

This picture of the battle was painted on deerskin by a Sioux Indian. It is called a pictograph.

4

Greasy Grass after the valley of thick prairie grasses that fed their horses and the buffalo they hunted.

The two names show what was important to the fighters on both sides of the battle. The Plains Indians needed the grasses that fed buffalo and horses and sustained the Plains way of life. White Americans, on the other hand, celebrated the efforts of a man whose battles against Native people spelled the end of that way of life.

A Turning Point

The Battle of the Little Bighorn was a turning point in the war of the white settlers against the Native people of the Plains. The Native Americans won the battle. After the battle, however, the U.S. government renewed its determination to defeat the Native people. Because of this, the white people won the war, and in the end the people of the Plains lost their homelands.

This July 1876 newspaper announced the Battle of the Little Bighorn to Americans about two weeks after the event.

Hoping for Fame and Glory

"In years long numbered with the past, when I was verging upon manhood, my every thought was ambitious—not to be wealthy, not to be learned, but to be great. I desired to link my name with a mark of honor—not only to the present, but to future generations."

George Armstrong Custer

Chapter One

The People of the Great Plains

This 1880 photo is of a Cheyenne tepee village near Fort Laramie in Wyoming. Cheyenne people lived on the western Plains.

The First People

Thousands of years ago, Native people moved across the North American continent and settled in all areas. By the time the English arrived in North America, the people already living there numbered in the millions.

The **descendants** of the first people of North America had their own cultures and languages. Their homes were in the mountains, deserts, valleys, and prairies. They lived in ways suited to the land and the climate of each region.

The Plains Indians

The Great Plains is a very big area that extends westward from the Mississippi River to the Rocky Mountains and runs north and south between the present-day borders of Canada and Mexico. This area has been inhabited by Native Americans, today known as the Plains Indians, for thousands of years.

Indians living on the Plains include the Arapaho, Cheyenne, Crow, Iowa, Pawnee, and Sioux. In the mid- to late 1800s, the Sioux were the strongest of the Plains people and had the most effective leaders. Their name came from a word for "treacherous snake" that had been given to them by their enemy, the Ojibwa people.

 ## The Tepee and Travois

The Plains people moved camp several times a year, and so they needed housing that could be dismantled, packed up, moved, and rebuilt in the new place. They lived in tepees, cone-shaped tents made from buffalo hide. The hides were stretched over long poles that came together at the top with an opening for smoke. This opening allowed people to heat their tents and cook in them.

When it was time to move camp, people tied their tent poles behind a horse and used the skins that formed the tent sides to make a sled they called a travois. Pulled behind horses, the travois could carry all their belongings.

A Blackfoot Sioux family travels across the northern Plains with small children and household goods in their two travois.

The Sioux people were a huge group and had three divisions: the Dakota, the Nakota, and the Lakota. The Sioux who fought at the Little Bighorn were the Lakota. There were seven Lakota groups. The Blackfoot, Brulé, Hunkpapa, Miniconjou, Oglala, Sans Arcs, and Two-Kettle—all these peoples were Lakota Sioux.

Hunting the Buffalo

The Indians of the Great Plains hunted antelope, deer, and elk, but most important to them was the buffalo. Buffalo meat was their main source of meat, but that is not all that the buffalo provided. The Sioux and other Plains people used buffalo hides to make tepees. They used fur and leather for clothes. They made tools and other useful things from the buffalo bones.

Because the buffalo was so important, the Plains people arranged their lives around the huge, shaggy animals. They lived a **nomadic** life, following the buffalo herds as they roamed the great stretches of the Plains.

Changes on the Plains

In the seventeenth century, a big change happened on the Plains when horses were introduced from the Southwest. The Plains Indians had never had horses before, but they knew a very good thing when they saw it. Within a few years, most groups had their own herds of horses. These horses quickly became their most valuable possessions, and the Plains people fought each other for them.

Hunting the buffalo on horseback instead of running alongside them on foot made a terrific improvement in the Plains Indians' hunting skills. They were able to keep up with the buffalo and were less likely to find themselves under the animals' hooves. Their skill with the lance and the bow and arrow kept the Plains Indians fed and warm.

In the eighteenth century, Spanish, French, and English people again transformed life on the Plains by introducing the gun. Now it was almost too easy to hunt the buffalo, and the herd sizes began to decrease. Plains people also used guns against their enemies.

Plains people depended for survival on hunting the buffalo that roamed in huge herds. This painting is by western artist Albert Bierstadt.

Warriors on the Plains developed rituals to show bravery in battle, including that of "counting coup." This was done by touching a fallen enemy, as shown here, or touching an opponent in battle without killing him.

A Warrior Culture

Even before white people came to the Plains, the Indians who lived there often fought each other over hunting grounds. Men who could fight well were given great honor, as in many other cultures, because they could protect the group. Even more importantly, they could protect their hunting grounds.

The White Man Comes to the Plains

In the 1800s, the people of the United States began to move west. At first, they mostly traveled through the Great Plains on their way to California and Oregon. There were scattered skirmishes with Plains people, but no major wars, because the whites were not trying to take the land.

By 1850, however, the goals of the government and the people had changed. Now they felt it was their right and duty to take over the whole continent. Already, a pattern of forcing the Indians to move, killing those who didn't, and making and breaking promises was well established. It was going to get much worse.

"Barbarous" Habits

"Our civilization ought to take the place of their **barbarous** habits. We claim the right to control the soil they occupy, and we assume that it is our duty to coerce them, if necessary, into the adoption and practice of our habits and customs."

Secretary of the Interior Columbus Delano, 1872, speaking about Native Americans

A group of settlers camp on the Plains during their journey to California. Travelers across Native lands were frequently helped by the Plains people, who acted as guides, traded horses, and supplied food.

Chapter Two

Broken Promises

The Sioux were angry because the U.S. Army built forts on their home-lands. This army post is Fort Abraham Lincoln in South Dakota. The Seventh Cavalry was based there under Lt. Col. Custer.

Conflict on the Plains

In 1865, the westward **migration** of white people began to increase. Among the newcomers were **prospectors** heading for the Montana gold fields. Their route, the Bozeman Trail, took them right through the homeland of the Sioux. When the U.S. government undertook to build a new road through the buffalo range, the Sioux rose up against the white people. This was not the first uprising of the Plains Indians, but now it was an all-out war.

Red Cloud

Red Cloud was a leader of the Oglala Sioux who had risen to power on the strength of a battle against Willliam Fetterman, a young **infantry** captain. Fetterman was based at Fort Phil Kearny in Montana. He had been heard to boast, "With eighty men I could ride through the Sioux **nation**." In December 1866, Red Cloud lured Fetterman and eighty of his men out of the fort. Red Cloud and his warriors killed all of them in an ambush.

For the next two years, Red Cloud, his Sioux warriors, and their Cheyenne allies fought against the soldiers on their land. Then, on August 2, 1868, Red Cloud led a thousand warriors in an attack against Fort Kearny. This time they lost badly, with over five hundred of Red Cloud's men killed. Many years later, Red Cloud still mourned their deaths. "I lost them," he said. "They never fought again."

The Treaty of Fort Laramie

After many battles and even more deaths, U.S. leaders were ready to stop fighting. They gave in to Red Cloud, agreeing to abandon the forts and stop work on the new road. The **treaty** they signed at Fort Laramie in 1868 allowed the Sioux to keep the Black Hills, a wooded hilly area in what are now South Dakota and Wyoming. The government promised the Sioux their land "for as long as the grass shall grow."

Promises
"They made us many promises, more than I can remember, but they never kept but one. They promised to take our land, and they took it."

Red Cloud

When Custer's expedition found gold in the Black Hills, prospectors poured into the area. Deadwood, South Dakota, shown here in 1876, was one of the boom-towns that soon appeared.

Custer on the Scene

George Armstrong Custer was already well known when he led an expedition of 1,200 men through the Black Hills in 1874. To the folks back home he was a dashing and brave "Indian fighter," a hero among men. To the Native people, he was the man who led the **massacre** of 103 sleeping Indians in a village on the Washita River in Oklahoma.

Custer was looking for a place to build a fort and to see if there was gold. He found both on Indian land. Within two years, there were 11,000 white people living there in a new

 George Armstrong Custer (1839–1876)

George Custer first won fame as an officer in the battles of the Civil War, when he was the youngest-ever brigadier general. His fame grew after the war as he led the Seventh Cavalry against the Plains Indians. The Indians called him "Yellow Hair" because of his long, blond hair. After the Little Bighorn, many people considered him a hero, but others thought that he led his men to certain death for his own glory.

town named Custer and many more in other **boomtowns** throughout the Black Hills. Although the Fort Laramie treaty had declared the land off-limits to whites, they soon outnumbered the Plains people.

Breaking the Treaty

The U.S. government badly wanted to take the Black Hills from the Indians. They tried to buy it, but the Indians would not sell it. In December 1875, President Grant ordered all Indians back to the **reservation**. They could no longer roam their free lands. The treaty was now officially broken.

Grant's order gave the Plains people six weeks to return to the reservation in the depths of winter. Many never even heard of the order, and others couldn't move their families that soon even if they wanted to. They were now considered hostile and the government made plans to capture them and force them onto the reservation. The stage was set for the Battle of the Little Bighorn.

This map shows the Bozeman Trail that cut through the Sioux's territory. It also shows how U.S. government treaties reduced Native lands piece by piece. Broken treaties reduced them even more.

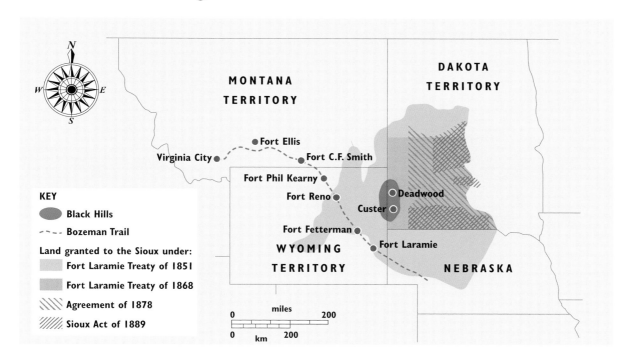

KEY
- Black Hills
- ---- Bozeman Trail

Land granted to the Sioux under:
- Fort Laramie Treaty of 1851
- Fort Laramie Treaty of 1868
- Agreement of 1878
- Sioux Act of 1889

15

Chapter Three

The Army Moves in

A Vanishing Way of Life

In 1876, the United States of America was one hundred years old with a population of over 44 million people. But there were only about 300,000 Native Americans left after European diseases and battles with settlers or soldiers had reduced or wiped out their communities.

The western Great Plains was one of the few areas where Native people still lived freely on their own land. Even there, however, life was changing. This was due in part to the slaying of millions of buffalo, mostly for sport, by white people. In just two years, over six million buffalo were killed. Their skeletons littered the Plains while Indians went hungry.

Sitting Bull (1831–1890)

Sitting Bull, or Tatanka Iyotake, was a Hunkpapa Sioux. All his life, he was determined not to be ruled by white people. Sitting Bull became the leading chief of the Sioux because he was so respected for his courage and wisdom. Years after the Battle of the Little Bighorn, Sitting Bull became a celebrity when he toured with Buffalo Bill's "Wild West Show" in the 1880s. In his final years, he had to live on a reservation, a way of life he hated.

General George Crook led his force from Fort Fetterman in Wyoming Territory. This picture shows some of his soldiers on their way to Rosebud Creek to find the Plains Indian camp.

A Gathering on the Plains

In 1876, Sioux Chief Sitting Bull brought his people together with other Plains Indians to celebrate their traditional way of life. Through the spring, Sioux, Cheyenne, and Arapaho left their reservations to answer Sitting Bull's call. By the end of June, over seven thousand people had gathered on Rosebud Creek in Montana Territory. Men, women, and children rejoiced in their freedom to live as they wanted.

The Army Plan

The United States Army, however, was already on its way to force the Indians back to the reservations. The plan was to lead soldiers in three groups to the Native encampment and attack from all sides.

Killing the Buffalo
"I can remember when the bison were so many that they could not be counted. But more and more [whites] came to kill them until they were only heaps of bones scattered where they used to be. The [white people] did not kill them to eat; they killed them for the metal that makes them crazy [gold, which they obtained by selling the buffalo hides]."

Sioux leader Black Elk

The U.S. Army's plan was to round up the Plains people by approaching the camp from three directions. But Crook's force from the south was stopped at the Battle of the Rosebud.

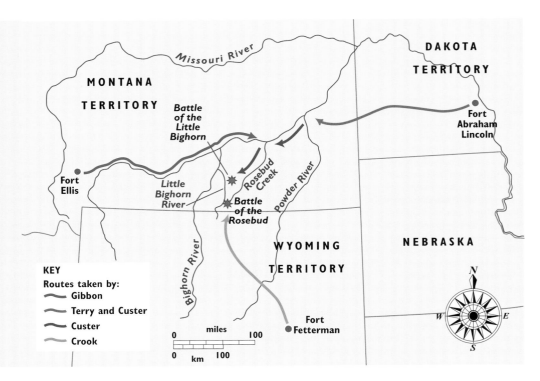

Battle of the Rosebud

The plan hit a snag. When General George Crook's force from the south approached Rosebud Creek, it was attacked on June 17, 1876, by Sioux war chief Crazy Horse and a thousand of his warriors. The battle was fierce and bloody, raging for six hours. When it was over, the Sioux left twenty soldiers dead and fifty-six wounded. Although they were only 20 miles (32 kilometers) from where they were to meet the other two army groups, Crook and his men retreated.

The Army Forces Meet

Meanwhile, Custer and his men, under General Alfred Terry, had made their way from Fort Abraham Lincoln to the place where Rosebud Creek and the Yellowstone River met. There they joined Colonel John Gibbon's force from the west.

The leaders learned that the Sioux camp had moved to somewhere along the Little Bighorn River. They decided that Gibbon and Terry would go west along the Yellowstone and then south to the Little Bighorn. Custer and his men would head south along Rosebud Creek and then march west to the Little Bighorn.

Custer Heads Out

On June 22, Custer set out with over six hundred men. Gibbon jokingly called out to Custer, "Now, Custer, don't be greedy, but wait for us." The call came back, "No, I will not."

On the night of June 24, **scouts** sighted the Indian camp at the Little Bighorn, still several miles away. At dawn on June 25, Custer climbed a hill overlooking the Little Bighorn. From his perch, he could see that the camp was far bigger than anyone had expected. Still, greedy for glory, he said to his troops, "The largest Indian camp on the North American continent is ahead and I'm going to attack it."

Custer's force in June 1876 included thirty-five Native scouts. In this picture from 1874, Custer is sitting in the middle with his favorite scout, Bloody Knife, sitting front left. Bloody Knife was killed at Little Bighorn.

Chapter Four

The Battle

Custer's Plan

On the morning of June 25, 1876, Custer's force approached the Native village. Custer made a plan to surround the camp by splitting his men into three groups.

When the first 140 men led by Major Marcus Reno reached the village from the south at about 3:00 P.M., a force of mounted warriors met them. Hundreds of warriors streamed toward them, overwhelming Reno and his men within minutes. With 40 dead and 13 wounded, the survivors retreated into the woods and then across the river to the high **bluffs**. They were joined there later by a second group of soldiers led by Captain Frederick Benteen.

This is a pictograph by Red Horse, a Sioux warrior who fought at the Battle of the Little Bighorn. It shows Custer's troops approaching the village.

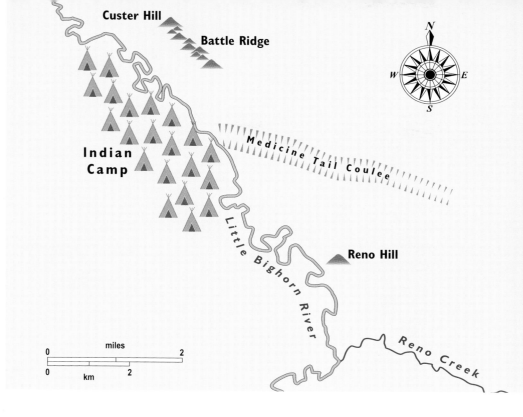

This map shows the Native camp by the Little Bighorn and Reno Hill, where Reno and Benteen's men ended up. It also shows Battle Ridge, where Custer's Last Stand took place,

Custer Advances

While Reno's men retreated from the Sioux south of the village, Custer and his men moved north to Medicine Tail **Coulee**. Custer saw what happened to Reno's unit, and he realized that what lay ahead was a very tough fight.

Custer split his forces again. He sent one group down toward the river and the village and another up the slope of the coulee. Within minutes, both groups were attacked.

At the River

The first group was fired on as they approached the river. Warriors concealed on the other side "rained lead across the river and drove the white **braves** back," according to Chief Sitting Bull. At first only a few warriors held off the soldiers. But they were soon joined by as many as 1,500 more. Led by Gall, a Sioux leader famous for his bravery, the warriors crossed the Little Bighorn and drove the soldiers back into the bluffs above the river.

21

This is a pictograph of the battle by Oglala Sioux Amos Bad Heart Bull. He shows Crazy Horse in the center, wearing spotted war paint.

Crazy Horse Strikes

Meanwhile, the war chief Crazy Horse roused the warriors in the village with a traditional battle cry: "Ho-ka hey! It is a good day to fight! It is a good day to die! Strong hearts, brave hearts, to the front! Weak hearts and cowards to the rear!"

Hundreds of warriors heeded his cry, heading to what later became known as Battle Ridge. Here, Custer and his remaining men had taken a position they hoped to defend

Crazy Horse (1840–1877)

Crazy Horse, or Tasunke Witko, was a great Sioux warrior and a thoughtful and brilliant leader. At the time of the battle, he was the war chief of all the Sioux. In May 1877, hunted by the U.S. Army, Crazy Horse surrendered. Later that year he was killed by soldiers. Someone had once asked him where his lands were, and Crazy Horse replied, "My lands are where my dead lie buried."

until reinforcements arrived. As Crazy Horse and his warriors streamed over the ridge, Gall and his men appeared from the other direction. Custer and his men were caught between the two Native forces.

On Battle Ridge

Nothing at all went well for Custer and his men. Forty of the soldiers shot their own horses so they could crouch behind them as they fought. Others ran into a deep coulee below the ridge, where they were trapped.

Indian survivors told of circling the soldiers on horseback, shooting them and their horses. One, Cheyenne Chief Two Moons, spoke of the bravery of the **bugler** who kept blowing commands until he was killed. When it was over, Chief Two Moons said, "All the soldiers were now killed, and the bodies were stripped. After that no one could tell which were officers."

The Last Stand

"It was said that up there . . . where the last stand took place, the Long Hair stood like a sheaf of corn with all the ears fallen around him. His hair was as the color of the grass when the frost comes."

Sitting Bull, 1877

This painting shows Custer's Last Stand, with Custer's men on the ridge surrounded by warriors.

The End of the Battle

After disposing of Custer and his men, the warriors turned their attention to Reno and Benteen's troops, who had retreated up to what is now called Reno Hill. The two sides fought until 9:00 P.M., when the warriors returned to their village. There they celebrated their victory, leaving the soldiers dug in on the hill.

The Indians returned on the morning of June 26. All day they circled and fired on the soldiers. At day's end, the Indians left the battlefield. That night, the Native camp broke up and the groups moved away. The battle was over.

This photograph, taken between 1877 and 1879, shows the battlefield at the Little Bighorn after the battle. Horse bones and soldiers' boots were still scattered on the hillside. Wooden markers showed where soldiers had died.

On the morning of June 27, General Terry and Colonel Gibbon and their men finally arrived at the battleground by the Little Bighorn River. There they discovered the gruesome remains of Custer and his men. It was Lieutenant J. H. Bradley, Gibbon's chief of scouts, who discovered Custer. He later wrote that Custer looked like "a man who has fallen asleep and enjoyed peaceful dreams." Like those of his men, Custer's body had been stripped of its clothes and weapons.

The Custers

George was not the only Custer who died at the battle. With him were his brothers Thomas, an army captain, and Boston, who was a guide. Also at the Little Bighorn were Custer's nephew Harry Reed and his brother-in-law James Calhoun.

Conclusion

A Battle Won, a War Lost

News of the Battle of the Little Bighorn spread across the country in early July. Many people called loudly for revenge. Thousands of soldiers chased the Indians across the Plains

until they had forced them back onto the reservations. The next year, Congress officially took the Black Hills away from the Sioux.

The government also stepped up its war against other Indians in the Pacific Northwest and in the Southwest. Within ten years, organized resistance to white settlement had ended.

In 1887, Sitting Bull and four hundred of his people fled to Canada, where they hoped they could live in peace. But the land and the weather were harsh, and in 1881 Sitting Bull surrendered so his people could be taken care of on a reservation. Sitting Bull gave himself up, saying, "Let it be recorded that I am the last man of my people to lay down my gun."

At the Little Bighorn battlefield, visitors can walk the hills dotted with white markers to show where soldiers fell.

The Little Bighorn Today

The Little Bighorn River still flows clear and cold. The lush, rolling hills surrounding it are still covered with the greasy grass that fed the buffalo, but the buffalo are long gone.

In the Black Hills, an image of Crazy Horse is being carved out of a mountain. Started in 1948, it will be the world's biggest sculpture when it is finished. The model in front is to show what the completed sculpture will look like.

For many years, the site of the Little Bighorn battle was preserved in memory of the Seventh Cavalry soldiers who died there. It was called the Custer Battlefield National Monument, and a stone monument was placed there to honor the soldiers. There was no memorial to reflect Indian losses.

In 1988, a group of Native people placed a plaque at the foot of the monument. The plaque says, "In Honor of our Indian patriots who fought and defeated the U.S. Cavalry in order to save our women and children from mass murder." Officials took it down, but it is in the battlefield museum. In 1992, the site was renamed the Little Bighorn Battlefield National Monument to honor the Native warriors as well as the white soldiers.

Common Goals
"All Americans— Indians and non-Indians—should continue to remember the events of June 25, 1876, but seek to narrow the differences which keep us from achieving our common goals."

U.S. Senator Ben Nighthorse, speaking at the 125th anniversary of the Little Bighorn, 2001

Time Line

1866	U.S. Army begins building three forts along the Bozeman Trail to protect travelers. December 21: Red Cloud and his warriors kill Captain William Fetterman and his men near Fort Phil Kearny.
1868	August 2: Red Cloud leads attack on Fort Phil Kearny; about 500 of his warriors are killed. November 9: Treaty of Fort Laramie ends Red Cloud's War. November 27: Attack by Lt. Col. George Armstrong Custer on Indian village by Washita River in Oklahoma.
1874	July 2–August 30: Custer leads an expedition that discovers gold in the Black Hills.
1875	December: U.S. government orders all Sioux to report to reservations by January 31, 1876.
1876	May 17: Custer leaves Fort Abraham Lincoln with General Alfred Terry. June 17: Sioux and Cheyenne attack General George Crook's troops at Rosebud Creek. June 22: Custer's unit moves toward the Little Bighorn River. June 25: Battle of the Little Bighorn. June 26: Plains people abandon siege at Reno Hill. June 27: General Terry and Colonel John Gibbon arrive at the Little Bighorn battlefield.
1877	U.S. government takes Black Hills away from Sioux people.
1940	Little Bighorn battlefield is named Custer Battlefield National Monument.
1948	Crazy Horse sculpture is started in Black Hills.
1992	Little Bighorn battlefield is renamed Little Bighorn Battlefield National Monument.

Things to Think About and Do

Living on the Plains

The Plains Indians and the white settlers had very different ways of living. Chapter One tells you about how Native American people lived on the Plains. Find out about how white settlers lived when they first came to the Plains. What were their homes like? What did they do to get food that was different from the Plains people? Draw pictures of a settler's home and of a Plains Indian's home. What are the differences and why?

Reasons to Fight

Imagine you are a U.S. cavalry soldier who took part in the Battle of the Little Bighorn. What were your reasons for fighting? Now imagine you are a Sioux warrior who fought at the battle. What were your reasons for fighting? Write a paragraph from each point of view.

At the Little Bighorn

You are ten years old and your family has followed Sitting Bull to the huge camp on the Little Bighorn River. Write a diary entry for three days in June 1876: the day before the battle, the day of the battle, and the day after, when your camp broke up and you and your family left. Describe what happened, what you heard and saw, and how you felt.

Glossary

barbarous:	wild and fierce, like a barbarian.
bluff:	steep bank or cliff above a river, lake, or coastline.
boomtown:	town that springs up quickly after a rush of people to one area, such as the towns appearing during the gold rushes of the 1800s.
brave:	Native American warrior.
bugler:	person who plays a bugle.
cavalry:	soldiers who travel and fight on horseback.
coulee:	small stream or streambed and the small ravine between two hills containing such a streambed.
descendant:	person who comes in a later generation in a family, such as a grandchild.
infantry:	soldiers who travel and fight on foot.
massacre:	killing of a group of people.
migration:	movement of people or animals from one place to another.
nation:	group of Native American people. Often used to mean large groups including many tribes, but can also mean one tribe.
nomadic:	traveling around as a way of life, rather than living in one place.
prospector:	person who explores an area looking for valuable resources such as gold or oil.
reservation:	public land set aside for Native American people to live on when they were removed from their homelands.
scout:	member of a group or army sent in advance to find out information, such as the whereabouts of an enemy.
treaty:	agreement made between people or groups of people after negotiation. Peace treaties are often made at the end of wars.

Further Information

Books

Birchfield, Don. *Crazy Horse* (*Raintree Biographies*). Raintree, 2002.

Marcovitz, Hal. *George Custer* (*Famous Figures of the American Frontier*). Chelsea House, 2001.

McGovern, Ann. *If You Lived with the Sioux Indians*. Scholastic, 1992.

Sita, Lisa. *Indians of the Great Plains: Traditions, History, Legends, and Life*. Gareth Stevens, 2001.

Viola, Herman J., ed. *It Is a Good Day to Die: Indian Eyewitnesses Tell the Story of the Battle of the Little Bighorn*. Bison Books, 2001.

Web Sites

www.crazyhorse.org Dedicated to the Crazy Horse Memorial, the huge statue being carved out of a mountain in the Black Hills.

www.mohicanpress.com/battles/ba04002.html Photographs of various sites at the Little Bighorn battlefield.

www.nps.gov/libi National Park Service web site with interesting information about the Little Bighorn Battlefield National Monument and maps and pictures of the battle.

Useful Addresses

Little Bighorn Battlefield National Monument
National Park Service
P.O. Box 39
Crow Agency, MT 59022
Telephone: (406) 638-2621

Index

Page numbers in **bold** indicate pictures.